THE COLLECTION

A Play in One Act

by Harold Pinter

∥SAMUEL FRENCH∥

samuelfrench.co.uk

FOR AMATEUR PRODUCTION ENQUIRIES

UNITED KINGDOM AND WORLD
EXCLUDING NORTH AMERICA
plays@samuelfrench.co.uk
020 7255 4302/01

Each title is subject to availability from Samuel French, depending upon country of performance.

THINKING ABOUT PERFORMING A SHOW?

There are thousands of plays and musicals available to perform from Samuel French right now, and applying for a licence is easier and more affordable than you might think

From classic plays to brand new musicals, from monologues to epic dramas, there are shows for everyone.

Plays and musicals are protected by copyright law so if you want to perform them, the first thing you'll need is a licence. This simple process helps support the playwright by ensuring they get paid for their work, and means that you'll have the documents you need to stage the show in public.

Not all our shows are available to perform all the time, so it's important to check and apply for a licence before you start rehearsals or commit to doing the show.

LEARN MORE & FIND THOUSANDS OF SHOWS

Browse our full range of plays and musicals and find out more about how to license a show

www.samuelfrench.co.uk/perform

Talk to the friendly experts in our Licensing team for advice on choosing a show, and help with licensing

plays@samuelfrench.co.uk   020 7387 9373

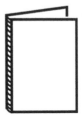

Other plays by HAROLD PINTER
published and licensed by Samuel French

Celebration

The Birthday Party

The Caretaker

The Dumb Waiter

Family Voices (from the collection *Other Places*)

The Homecoming

A Kind of Alaska (from the collection *Other Places*)

The Lover

Mixed Doubles

Mountain Language

A Night Out

One for the Road (from the collection *Other Places*)

One to Another

The Room

A Slight Ache

Victoria Station (from the collection *Other Places*)

**Other plays by HAROLD PINTER
licensed by Samuel French**

Apart from That

Ashes to Ashes

The Basement

Betrayal

The Black and White

The Dwarfs

The Hothouse

Landscape

Last To Go

Monologue

Moonlight

The New World Order

Night School

No Man's Land

Old Times

Party Time

Precisely

Press Conference

Request Stop

Silence

Tess

That's All

That's Your Trouble

Trouble in the Works

FIND PERFECT PLAYS TO PERFORM AT
www.samuelfrench.co.uk/perform

ABOUT THE AUTHOR

Harold Pinter was born in London in 1930. He lived with
Antonia Fraser from 1975 until his death on Christmas Eve
2008. (They were married in 1980).

After studying at the Royal Academy of Dramatic Art and the
Central School of Speech and Drama, he worked as an actor
under the stage name David Baron. Following his success as a
playwright, he continued to act under his own name, on stage
and screen. He last acted in 2006 when he appeared in Beckett's
Krapp's Last Tape at the Royal Court Theatre, directed by Ian
Rickson.

He wrote twenty-nine plays including *The Birthday Party, The
Dumb Waiter, A Slight Ache, The Hothouse, The Caretaker, The
Collection, The Lover, The Homecoming, Old Times, No Man's
Land, Betrayal, A Kind of Alaska, One For The Road, The New
World Order, Moonlight* and *Ashes to Ashes*. Sketches include
*The Black and White, Request Stop, That's your Trouble, Night,
Precisely, Apart From that* and the recently rediscovered,
Umbrellas.

He directed twenty-seven theatre productions, including James
Joyce's *Exiles*, David Mamet's *Oleanna*, seven plays by Simon
Gray (one of which was *Butley* in 1971 which he directed the
film of three years later) and many of his own plays including his
last, *Celebration*, paired with his first, *The Room* at The Almeida
Theatre, London in the spring of 2000.

He wrote twenty-one screenplays including *The Pumpkin Eater,
The Servant, The Go-Between, The French Lieutenant's Woman*
and *Sleuth*.

In 2005 he received the Nobel Prize for Literature. Other
awards include the Companion of Honour for services to
Literature, the Legion D'Honneur, the European Theatre Prize
the Laurence Olivier Award and the Moliere D'Honneur for
lifetime achievement. In 1999 he was made a Companion of
Literature by the Royal Society of Literature. Harold Pinter was
awarded eighteen honorary degrees.

THE COLLECTION

Produced by the Royal Shakespeare Company at the Aldwych
Theatre, London, on the 18th June 1962, with the following
cast of characters:

(in the order of their appearance)

HARRY	Michael Hordern
STELLA	Barbara Murray
JAMES	Kenneth Haigh
BILL	John Ronane

Directed by Peter Hall and Harold Pinter

Setting by Paul Anstee and John Bury

*The action of the play passes in Harry's house in Belgravia
and James' flat in Chelsea*

Time – the present

SCENE—HARRY's *house in Belgravia and* JAMES' *flat in Chelsea. An autumn evening.*

The stage is divided into three areas, two peninsulas and a promontory. Each area is distinct and separate from the other. HARRY's *house is left. The décor is elegant with period furnishing. This setting comprises the living-room and the hall with the front door and staircase to the first floor. There is an exit to the kitchen below the staircase. In the living-room there is a small round table centre, with carver chairs right and left of it. A sideboard for drinks is left. A console table stands up centre, with brackets for ornaments on the wall behind it. A pouffe stands right and a fender and fire-irons down centre, indicate the fireplace. A low-backed fireside chair is down left with a small occasional table left of it. A telephone is on the console table up centre. There is a hatstand in the hall, below the stairs.*

JAMES' *flat is right. This setting, on a low rostrum, shows the living-room with tasteful, contemporary furnishings. The front door and other rooms are off right. Up right centre is a long sofa with a low coffee-table in front of it. An upholstered armchair stands left, with a small occasional table above it. A long, low radiogram is down left centre with a record cabinet right of it. Up left centre in the street outside the front door to* HARRY's *house there is a "promontory" with a telephone-box.*

When the curtain rises, it is late at night. The rooms are in darkness. The hall area is lit. It is moonlight in the street up left centre and the telephone-box interior light is on. The figure of JAMES, *unrecognized by the audience, can be dimly observed inside the telephone-box, with his*

back to the audience. The telephone in **HARRY**'s *house
left is ringing.* **HARRY**, *a man in his forties, enters up
centre in the street, opens the front door of his house,
goes into the hall, closes the door and switches on the
lights. The lights come up on the room left.* **HARRY** *moves
to the telephone and lifts the receiver.*

HARRY *(into the telephone)* Hullo?

JAMES' *voice is heard.*

JAMES *(through the telephone)* Is that you, Bill?

HARRY No, he's in bed. Who's this?

JAMES In bed?

HARRY Who is this?

JAMES What's he doing in bed?

There is a pause.

HARRY Do you know it's four o'clock in the morning?

JAMES Well, give him a nudge. Tell him I want a word with him.

There is a pause.

HARRY Who is this?

JAMES Go and wake him up, there's a good boy.

There is a pause.

HARRY Are you a friend of his?

JAMES He'll know me when he sees me.

HARRY Oh, yes?

There is a pause.

JAMES Aren't you going to wake him?

HARRY No, I'm not.

There is a pause.

JAMES Tell him I'll be in touch.

JAMES *replaces the receiver, leaves the telephone-box and exits up right. The light in the box goes out.*

HARRY *replaces his receiver, goes slowly into the hall, switches off the lights and exits up the stairs. The lights fade in the room left, in the hall and in the street and come up on the room right. It is morning.*

JAMES, *a man in his thirties, enters down right. He is casually dressed and is smoking a cigarette. He sits on the sofa and picks up a cup of coffee from the table in front of him.*

STELLA, *a woman in her thirties, enters down right, carrying her coat. She drops the coat on to the sofa, goes to the radiogram, picks up her gloves and puts them on. She picks up her purse and handbag from the radiogram, looks in the purse, puts it in the handbag then takes a bracelet from the bag, puts the bag on the radiogram and fixes the bracelet on her wrist. She then takes a perfume atomizer from the bag, uses it on her throat and replaces it in the bag. There is a silence.*

STELLA I'm going. *(She pauses)* Aren't you coming in today?

JAMES *(after a pause)* No. *(He puts down his cup)*

STELLA You had to meet those people from...

There is a pause. JAMES *sits still.*

(she moves slowly to the sofa, picks up her coat, puts it on, then turns to JAMES*)* You had to meet those people about that order. Shall I phone them when I get to the shop?

JAMES You could do—yes.

STELLA What are you going to do?

JAMES *looks at her, with a brief smile, then looks away.*

Jimmy... *(She pauses and collects her handbag)* Are you going out? *(She pauses)* Will you—be in tonight?

JAMES *reaches for a glass ashtray, flicks his ash into it and regards the ashtray.*

STELLA *turns and exits down right. The front door is heard to slam.* JAMES *continues regarding the ashtray. The lights on the room right fade to half. The lights come up on the room left and the hall. It is morning.*

BILL, *a man in his late twenties, enters from the kitchen left carrying a tray with breakfast for two, and a newspaper. He puts the tray on the table, arranges the breakfast things, sits right of the table, props the newspaper on the toast rack, reads and sips his fruit juice.*

HARRY, *in his dressing-goom, enters down the stairs, trips on them and stumbles.*

BILL *(looking up)* What have you done?

HARRY I tripped on that stair rod. *(He comes into the room)*

BILL All right?

HARRY It's that stair rod. I thought you said you were going to fix it.

BILL I did fix it.

HARRY Well, you didn't fix it very well. *(He sits left of the table and holds his head)* Ooh.

BILL *pours tea.*

JAMES, *in the room right, stubs out his cigarette, rises and exits right. The lights on the room right fade.*

(he sips his tea, puts down the cup and looks at the table) Where's my fruit juice? I haven't had my fruit juice.

BILL *reaches behind his newspaper and passes a glass of fruit juice to* **HARRY.**

What's it doing over there? *(He sips the fruit juice)* What's this? Pineapple?

BILL Grapefruit.

There is a pause.

HARRY I'm sick and tired of that stair rod. Why don't you screw it in or something? You're supposed—you're supposed to be able to use your hands.

There is a pause.

BILL What time did you get in?

HARRY Four.

BILL Good party?

HARRY *(after a pause)* You didn't make any toast this morning.

BILL No. Do you want some?

HARRY No, I don't.

BILL I can if you like.

HARRY It's all right. Don't bother.

There is a pause.

How are you spending your day today?

BILL Go and see a film, I think.

HARRY Wonderful life you lead. *(He pauses and sips his tea)* Do you know some maniac telephoned you last night?

BILL *looks at* **HARRY.**

Just as I got in. Four o'clock. Walked in the door and the telephone was ringing.

BILL Who was it?

HARRY I've no idea.

BILL What did he want?

HARRY You. He was shy, wouldn't tell me his name. Who could it have been?

BILL I've no idea.

HARRY He was very insistent. Said he was going to get in touch again. *(He pauses)* Who the hell was it?

BILL I've just said—I haven't the remotest idea.

There is a pause.

HARRY Did you meet anyone last week?

BILL Meet anyone? What do you mean?

HARRY I mean, could it have been anyone you met? You must have met lots of people.

BILL I didn't speak to a soul.

HARRY Must have been miserable for you.

BILL I was only there one night, wasn't I? *(He picks up the teapot)* Some more?

HARRY No, thank you.

BILL pours tea for himself. The lights come up to half on the telephone-box.

JAMES, in an overcoat, enters up right and goes into the box. The light in the box comes on. BILL reads his paper.

I must shave. *(He looks at BILL)*

There is a pause.

BILL *(looking up)* Mmmmn?

There is a silence.

HARRY *rises, goes into the hall and exits up the stairs.*

BILL *reads. After a moment, the telephone rings.* BILL *rises, goes to the telephone and lifts the receiver.*

(into the telephone) Hallo?

JAMES' *voice is heard.*

JAMES *(through the telephone)* Is that you, Bill?

BILL Yes?

JAMES Are you in?

BILL Who's this?

JAMES Don't move. I'll be straight round.

BILL What do you mean? Who is this?

JAMES About two minutes. All right?

BILL I'm sorry—you can't do that. I've got some people here.

JAMES Never mind. We can go into another room.

BILL This is ridiculous. Do I know you?

JAMES You'll know me when you see me.

BILL Do you know me?

JAMES Just stay where you are. I'll be right round.

BILL But what do you want? Who...? You can't do that, I'm going straight out, I won't be in.

JAMES See you.

JAMES *replaces the receiver, leaves the telephone-box and exits left. The light in the box goes out.*

BILL *replaces his receiver, goes into the hall, puts on his overcoat, swift but not hurried, goes out of the front door and exits right.*

HARRY *(offstage upstairs; calling)* Bill, was that you?

HARRY *enters on the stairs.*

(he calls) Bill.

HARRY *comes down the stairs, treads carefully over the stair rod, goes into the living-room, looks around then collects the breakfast things and exits with the tray to the kitchen.*

JAMES *enters left in the street, comes to the front door and rings the bell.*

HARRY *enters from the kitchen, goes into the hall and opens the front door.*

Yes?

JAMES I'm looking for Bill Lloyd.

HARRY He's out. Can I help?

JAMES When will he be in?

HARRY I can't say. Does he know you?

JAMES I'll try some other time, then.

HARRY Well, perhaps you'd like to leave your name. I can tell him when I see him.

JAMES No, that's all right. Just tell him I called.

HARRY Tell him who called?

JAMES Sorry to bother you. *(He turns to go)*

HARRY Just a minute.

JAMES *stops and turns.*

You're not the man who telephoned last night, are you?

JAMES Last night?

HARRY You didn't telephone early this morning?

JAMES No—sorry...

HARRY Well, what do you want?

JAMES I'm looking for Bill.

HARRY You didn't by any chance telephone just now?

JAMES I think you've got the wrong man.

HARRY I think you have.

JAMES I don't think you know anything about it.

JAMES turns and exits up right.

HARRY watches him go then closes the door and exits up the stairs. The lights in the room left fade. The light in the street fades. Lights came up on the room right for moonlight effect. The front door is heard to slam. The hall light off right comes on.

STELLA enters right, crosses to the table-lamp and switches it on. The lights come up on the room right to half. STELLA removes her coat and puts it on the sofa, then looks off right.

STELLA *(calling)* Jimmy? *(She listens)*

There is silence.

STELLA puts down her handbag, goes to the radiogram, puts on a record and switches it on. It is cool jazz. She then picks up her coat and exits right. The lights come up on the room and hall left. It is night.

BILL enters left from the kitchen, carrying some magazines which he throws on the floor down centre. He goes to the sideboard, pours a drink, picks up the glasses, moves centre, lies on the floor, puts the drink beside him and flicks through a magazine.

HARRY *enters down the stairs, goes out of the front door and exits up right.*

STELLA *enters right, carrying a white Persian kitten. She lies on the sofa, nuzzling the kitten. The hall light right goes out.*

JAMES *enters the street from left, goes to the front door and rings the bell. The lights on the room right dim a little. The music fades out.* **BILL** *rises, picks up his glass, puts it on the table, goes into the hall and opens the front door.*

BILL Yes?

JAMES Bill Lloyd?

BILL Yes?

JAMES *(after a pause)* Oh, I'd—I'd like to have a word with you.

BILL *(after a pause)* I'm sorry, I don't think I know you.

JAMES Don't you?

BILL No.

JAMES Well, there's something I'd like to talk to you about.

BILL I'm terribly sorry, I'm busy.

JAMES It won't take long.

BILL I'm awfully sorry. Perhaps you'd like to put it down on paper and send it to me.

JAMES That's not possible.

There is a pause.

BILL *(closing the door)* Do forgive me...

JAMES *(putting his foot in the door)* Look, I want to speak to you.

There is a long pause.

BILL Did you phone me today?

JAMES That's right. I called, but you'd gone out.

BILL You called here? I didn't know that.

JAMES I think I'd better come in, don't you?

BILL You can't just barge into someone's house like this, you know. What do you want?

JAMES Why don't you stop wasting your time and let me in?

BILL I could call the police.

JAMES Not worth it.

They stare at each other.

BILL All right. *(He stands aside)*

JAMES enters the hall and goes into the living-room. BILL closes the front door and follows JAMES in. JAMES looks about the room.

JAMES Got any olives?

BILL How did you know my name?

JAMES No olives?

BILL Olives? I'm afraid not.

JAMES You mean to say you don't keep olives for your guests?

BILL You're not my guest, you're an intruder. What can I do for you?

JAMES Do you mind if I sit down?

BILL Yes, I do.

JAMES You'll get over it. *(He sits right of the table, then rises, removes his coat, puts it over the back of his chair then resumes his seat)*

BILL What's your name, old boy?

JAMES reaches to a bowl of fruit, takes a grape and eats it.

JAMES Where shall I put the pips?

BILL In your wallet.

JAMES takes out his wallet and deposits the pips.

JAMES *(regarding* **BILL***)* You're not a bad-looking bloke.

BILL Oh, thanks.

JAMES You're not a film star, but you're quite tolerable looking, I suppose.

BILL That's more than I can say for you.

JAMES I'm not interested in what you can say for me.

BILL To put it quite bluntly, old chap, I'm even less interested than you are. Now look, come on, please, what do you want?

JAMES rises, crosses to the sideboard and stares at the bottles. **STELLA***, in the room right, rises with the kitten and exits slowly right, nuzzling it. The lights fade on the room right.* **JAMES** *pours a whisky for himself.* **BILL** *moves right.*

Cheers.

JAMES *(crossing to left of* **BILL***)* Did you have a good time in Leeds last week?

BILL What?

JAMES Did you have a good time in Leeds last week?

BILL Leeds?

JAMES Did you enjoy yourself?

BILL What makes you think I was in Leeds?

JAMES Tell me all about it. See much of the town? Get out to the country at all?

BILL What are you talking about?

There is a pause. **JAMES** *crosses to the chair down left and sits.*

JAMES *(with fatigue)* Aaah. You were down there for the dress collection. You took some of your models.

BILL Did I?

JAMES You stayed at the *Westbury Hotel.*

BILL Oh?

JAMES Room one-four-two.

BILL One-four-two? Oh. Was it comfortable?

JAMES Comfortable enough.

BILL Oh, good.

JAMES Well, you had your yellow pyjamas with you.

BILL Did I, really? What, the ones with the black initials?

JAMES Yes, you had them on you in one-six-five.

BILL In what?

JAMES One-six-five.

BILL One-six-five? I thought I was in one-four-two.

JAMES You looked into one-four-two. But you didn't stay there.

BILL Well, that's a bit silly, isn't it? Booking a room and not staying in it.

JAMES One-six-five is just along the passage to one-four-two, you're not far away.

BILL Oh, well, that's a relief.

JAMES You could easily nip back to shave.

BILL From one-six-five?

JAMES Yes.

BILL What was I doing there?

JAMES *(casually)* My wife was in there. That's where you slept with her.

There is a silence.

BILL Well—who told you that?

JAMES She did.

BILL You should have her seen to.

JAMES Be careful.

BILL Mmmm? Who is your wife?

JAMES You know her.

BILL I don't think so.

JAMES No?

BILL No, I don't think so at all.

JAMES I see.

BILL I was nowhere near Leeds last week, old chap. Nowhere near your wife, either, I'm quite sure of that. Apart from that, I—just don't do such things. Not in my book. *(He pauses)* I wouldn't dream of it. Well, I think that closes the subject, don't you?

JAMES Come here. I want to tell you something.

BILL I'm expecting guests in a minute, you know. Cocktails. I'm standing for Parliament next season.

JAMES Come here.

BILL I'm going to be Minister for Home Affairs.

JAMES *rises and crosses to* **BILL.**

JAMES *(confidentially)* When you treat my wife like a whore, then I think I'm entitled to know what you've got to say about it.

BILL But I don't know your wife.

JAMES You do. You met her at ten o'clock last Friday in the lounge. You fell into conversation, you bought her a couple of drinks, you went upstairs together in the lift. In the lift you never took your eyes from her, you found you were both on the same floor, you helped her out, by her arm. You stood with her in the corridor, looking at her. You touched her shoulder, said good night, went to your room, she went to hers, you changed into your yellow pyjamas and black dressing-gown, you went down the passage and knocked on her door, you'd left your toothpaste in town. She opened the door, you went in, she was still dressed. You admired the room, it was so feminine, you felt awake, didn't feel like sleeping, you sat down on the bed. *(He crosses to the pouffe)* She wanted you to go, you wouldn't. She became upset, you sympathized, away from home, on business, horrible life, especially for a woman. You comforted her, you gave her solace, you stayed.

BILL *(after a pause)* Look, do you mind—just going off, now? You're giving me a bit of a headache.

JAMES *(sitting on the pouffe)* You knew she was married—why did you feel it necessary—to do that?

BILL She must have known she was married, too. Why did she feel it necessary—to do that?

There is a pause.

(with a chuckle) That's got you, hasn't it? *(He pauses, crosses to the sideboard, takes a cigarette from a box and lights it)* Well, look, it's really just a lot of rubbish. You know that. *(He moves to the chair down left and sits)* Is she supposed to have resisted me at all?

JAMES A little.

BILL Only a little?

JAMES Yes.

BILL Do you believe her?

JAMES Yes.

BILL Everything she says?

JAMES Sure.

BILL Did she bite at all?

JAMES No.

BILL Scratch?

JAMES A little.

BILL You've got a devoted wife, haven't you? Keeps you very well-informed, right up to the minutest detail. She scratched a little, did she? Where? *(He holds up his hand)* On the hand? No scar. No scar anywhere. Absolutely unscarred. We can go before a Commissioner for Oaths, if you like. I'll strip, show you my unscarred body. Yes, what we need is an independent witness. You got any chambermaids on your side or anything?

JAMES *applauds briefly.*

JAMES You're a wag, aren't you? I never thought you'd be such a wag. You've really got a sense of fun. You know what I'd call you?

BILL What?

JAMES A wag.

BILL Oh, thanks very much.

JAMES No, I'm glad to pay a compliment when a compliment's due. *(He rises and crosses to the sideboard)* What about a drink?

BILL That's good of you.

JAMES What will you have?

BILL *(rising and crossing to centre)* Got any vodka?

JAMES Let's see. Yes, I think we can find you some vodka.

BILL Oh, scrumptious.

JAMES *(turning)* Say that again.

BILL What?

JAMES That word.

BILL What— "scrumptious"?

JAMES That's it.

BILL Scrumptious.

JAMES Marvellous. *(He pours a drink for* **BILL** *and refills his own glass)* You probably remember that from school, don't you?

BILL Now that you mention it I think you might be right.

JAMES I thought I was. *(He crosses and hands* **BILL** *his drink)* Here's your vodka.

BILL That's very generous of you.

JAMES Not at all. Cheers.

BILL Cheers.

They drink. **BILL** *moves right.*

JAMES Eh, come here.

BILL What?

JAMES I bet you're a wow at parties.

BILL Well, it's nice of you to say so, but I wouldn't say I was all that much of a wow.

JAMES Go on, I bet you are.

BILL *(after a pause)* You think I'm a wow, do you?

JAMES At parties, I should think you are.

BILL No, I'm not much of a wow, really. The bloke I share this house with is, though.

JAMES *(moving slowly to* **BILL***)* Oh, I met him. Looked a jolly kind of chap.

BILL Yes, he's very good at parties. Bit of a conjuror.

JAMES What—rabbits?

BILL Well, not so much rabbits, no.

JAMES No rabbits?

BILL No. He doesn't like rabbits, actually. They give him hay fever.

JAMES Poor chap.

BILL Yes, it is a pity.

JAMES Seen a doctor about it?

BILL Oh, he's had it since he was that high.

JAMES Brought up in the country, I suppose?

BILL In a manner of speaking, yes. *(He pauses)* Ah, well, it's been very nice meeting you, old chap. You must come again when the weather's better.

JAMES makes a sudden move forward. **BILL** *starts back and falls over the pouffe, flat on to the floor.* **JAMES** *chuckles.*

(after a pause) You've made me spill my drink. You've made me spill it on my cardigan.

JAMES *stands over him.*

I could easily kick you from here. *(He pauses)* Are you going to let me get up? *(He pauses)* Are you going to let me get up? *(He pauses)* Now, listen—I'll tell you what— *(He pauses)* if you let me get up... *(He pauses)* I'm not very comfortable. *(He pauses)* If you let me get up—I'll—I'll tell you—the truth.

JAMES *(after a pause)* Tell me the truth from there.

BILL No. No, when I'm up.

JAMES Tell me from there.

There is a pause.

BILL Oh, well. I'm only telling you because I'm utterly bored. The truth—is that it never happened—what you said, anyway. I didn't know she was married. She never told me. Never said a word. But nothing of that—happened, I can assure you. All that happened was—you were right, actually, about going up in the lift—we—got out of the lift, and then suddenly she was in my arms. Really wasn't my fault, nothing was farther from my mind, biggest surprise of my life, must have found me terribly attractive quite suddenly, I don't know—but I—I didn't refuse. Anyway, we just kissed a bit, only a few minutes, by the lift, no-one about, and that was that, she went to her room. *(He props himself up on the pouffe)* The rest of it just didn't happen. I mean, I wouldn't do that sort of thing. I mean, that sort of thing—it's just meaningless. I can understand that you're upset, of course, but honestly, there was nothing else to it. Just a few kisses. *(He rises, wiping his cardigan)* I'm dreadfully sorry, really. I mean, I've no idea why she should make up all that. Pure fantasy. Really rather naughty of her. *(He moves down left)* Rather alarming. *(He pauses)* Do you know her well?

JAMES And then about midnight you went into her private bathroom and had a bath. You sang *Coming Through the Rye*. You used her bath towel. Then you walked about the room with her bath towel, pretending you were a Roman.

BILL Did I?

JAMES Then I phoned. *(He pauses)* I spoke to her. Asked her how she was. She said she was all right. Her voice was a little low. I asked her to speak up. She didn't have much to say. You were sitting on the bed, next to her.

There is a silence.

BILL Not sitting. Lying.

The lights on the room left and in the hall blackout. Church bells are heard. During the blackout JAMES *crosses to the room right.* HARRY *enters from the kitchen with the breakfast tray and puts it on the table.* BILL *puts on a dressing-gown. The lights come up on the room right, on the room left and the hall. It is Sunday morning.* JAMES *is seated on the sofa in the room right, reading a newspaper. In the room left,* BILL *is seated right of the table, reading a newspaper.* HARRY *is seated left of the table, watching* BILL. *After a few moments, the church bells cease.*

HARRY Put the paper down.

BILL What?

HARRY Put it down.

BILL Why?

HARRY You've read it.

BILL No, I haven't. There's lots to read, you know.

HARRY I told you to put it down.

BILL looks at HARRY, throws the paper at him, coolly, and rises. HARRY picks up the paper and reads it.

BILL Oh, you just wanted it yourself, did you?

HARRY Want it? I don't want it. *(He deliberately crumples the paper and drops it)* I don't want it. Do you want it?

BILL You're being a little erratic this morning, aren't you?

HARRY Am I?

BILL I would say you were.

HARRY Well, you know what it is, don't you?

BILL No.

HARRY It's the church bells. You know how church bells always set me off. You know how they affect me.

BILL I never hear them.

HARRY You're not the sort of person who would, are you?

BILL I'm finding all this faintly idiotic. *(He bends to pick up the paper)*

HARRY Don't touch that paper.

BILL Why not?

HARRY Don't touch it.

> **BILL** *stares at* **HARRY** *then slowly picks up the paper. There is a silence.*

BILL *(tossing the paper to* **HARRY***)* You have it. I don't want it.

> **BILL** *exits up the stairs.* **HARRY** *opens the paper and reads.*

> **STELLA** *enters the room right, carrying a tray with coffee and biscuits. She puts the tray on the coffee-table, sits right of* **JAMES** *on the sofa, pours the coffee, puts a cup in front of* **JAMES***, then sips her own coffee.*

STELLA Would you like a biscuit?

JAMES No, thank you.

STELLA *(after a pause)* I'm going to have one.

JAMES You'll get fat.

STELLA From biscuits?

JAMES You don't want to get fat, do you?

STELLA Why not?

JAMES Perhaps you do.

STELLA It's not one of my aims.

JAMES What is your aim? *(He pauses)* I'd like an olive.

STELLA Olive? We haven't got any.

JAMES How do you know?

STELLA I know.

JAMES Have you looked?

STELLA I don't need to look, do I? I know what I've got.

JAMES You know what you've got? *(He pauses)* Why haven't we got any olives?

STELLA I didn't know you liked them.

JAMES That must be the reason we've never had them in the house. You've simply never been interested enough in olives to ask me whether I liked them or not.

The telephone left rings. HARRY *drops the paper, rises, goes to the telephone and lifts the receiver.*

BILL *enters down the stairs and goes slowly into the living-room.*

HARRY *(into the telephone)* Hullo?

VOICE *(through the telephone)* Is that BEL four-six-five-o?

HARRY What? No. Wrong number. *(He replaces the receiver and turns to* BILL*)* Wrong number. Who do you think it was?

BILL I didn't think. *(He picks up the paper and sits on the chair down left)*

HARRY *(sitting left of the table)* Oh, by the way, a chap called for you yesterday.

BILL Oh, yes?

HARRY Just after you'd gone out.

BILL Oh, yes?

HARRY *(rising)* Ah, well, time for the joint. *(He picks up the breakfast tray)* Roast or chips?

BILL I don't want any potatoes, thank you.

HARRY No potatoes? What an extraordinary thing.

> HARRY *exits to the kitchen with the tray, re-enters immediately, takes a cigarette from the box on the sideboard, lights it then sits left of the table.*

Yes, this chap, he was asking for you, he wanted you.

BILL What for?

HARRY He wanted to know if you ever cleaned your shoes with furniture polish.

BILL Really? How odd.

HARRY Not odd. Some kind of national survey.

BILL What did he look like?

HARRY Oh—lemon hair, nigger-brown teeth, wooden leg, bottle-green eyes—and a toupee. Know him?

BILL Never met him.

HARRY You'd know him if you saw him.

BILL I doubt it.

HARRY What, a man who looked like that?

BILL Plenty of men look like that.

HARRY That's true. That's very true. The only thing is that this particular man was here last night.

BILL Was he? I didn't see him.

HARRY Oh, yes, he was here, but I've got a funny feeling he wore a mask. It was the same man but he wore a mask, that's all there is to it. He didn't dance here last night, did he, or do any gymnastics?

BILL No-one danced here last night.

HARRY Aah! Well, that's why you didn't notice his wooden leg. I couldn't help seeing it myself when he came to the front door because he stood on the top step stark naked. Didn't seem very cold, though. He had a water-bottle under his arm instead of a hat.

BILL Those church bells have certainly left their mark on you.

HARRY They haven't helped, but the fact of the matter is, old chap, that I don't like strangers coming into my house without an invitation. *(He pauses)* Who is this man and what does he want?

There is a pause. BILL *rises.*

BILL Will you excuse me? I really think it's about time I was dressed, don't you?

BILL *exits up the stairs, taking the paper with him.*

HARRY, *after a moment, rises and follows* BILL *off up the stairs. The lights on the room left and the hall fade. In the room right,* JAMES *is reading.* STELLA *is sitting silently.*

STELLA *(after a pause)* What do you think about going for a run today—in the country?

There is a pause. JAMES *puts the paper down.*

JAMES I've come to a decision.

STELLA What?

JAMES I'm going to go and see him.

STELLA See him? Who? *(She pauses)* What for?

JAMES Oh—have a chat with him.

STELLA What's the point of doing that?

JAMES I feel I'd like to.

STELLA I just don't see—what there is to be gained. What's the point of it? *(She pauses)* What are you going to do—hit him?

JAMES No, no. I'd just like to hear what he's got to say.

STELLA Why?

JAMES I want to know what his attitude is.

STELLA *(after a pause)* He doesn't matter.

JAMES What do you mean?

STELLA He's not important.

JAMES Do you mean anyone would have done? You mean it just happened to be him, but it might as well have been anyone?

STELLA No. *(She sips her coffee)*

JAMES What then?

STELLA Of course it couldn't have been anyone. It was him. It was just—something...

JAMES That's what I mean. It was him. That's why I think he's worth having a look at. I want to see what he's like. It'll be instructive, educational.

There is a pause. STELLA *puts her cup down.*

STELLA Please don't go and see him. You don't know where he lives, anyway.

JAMES You don't think I should see him?

STELLA It won't—make you feel any better.

JAMES I want to see if he's changed.

STELLA What do you mean?

JAMES I want to see if he's changed from when I last saw him. He may have gone down the drain since I last saw him. I must say he looked in good shape, though.

STELLA You've never seen him. *(She pauses)* You don't know him. *(She pauses)* You don't know where he lives. *(She pauses)* When did you see him?

JAMES We had dinner together last night.

STELLA What?

JAMES Splendid host.

STELLA I don't believe it.

JAMES Ever been to his place? *(He pauses)* Rather nice. Ever been there?

STELLA I met him in Leeds, that's all.

JAMES Oh, is that all? Well, we'll have to go round there one night. The grub's good, I can't deny it. I found him quite charming. *(He pauses)* He remembered the occasion well. He was perfectly frank. You know—a man's man. Straight from the shoulder. He entirely confirmed your story.

STELLA Did he?

JAMES Mmm. Only thing—he rather implied that you led him on. Typical masculine thing to say, of course.

STELLA That's a lie.

JAMES You know what men are. I reminded him that you'd resisted, that you'd hated the whole thing, but that you'd been—how can we say—somehow hypnotized by him, it happens sometimes. He agreed it can happen sometimes. He told me he'd been hypnotized once by a cat. Wouldn't go into any more details, though. Still, I must admit we rather hit it off. We've got the same interests. He was most amusing over the brandy.

STELLA I'm not interested.

JAMES In fact he was most amusing over the whole thing.

STELLA Was he?

JAMES But especially over the brandy. He's got the right attitude, you see. As a man, I can only admire it.

STELLA What is his attitude?

JAMES What's your attitude?

STELLA I don't know what you're—I just don't know what you're—I just—hoped you'd understand. *(She covers her face, crying)*

JAMES Well, I do understand, but only after meeting him. Now I'm perfectly happy. I can see it both ways, three ways, all ways—every way. It's perfectly clear, there's nothing to it, everything's back to normal. The only difference is that I've come across a man I can respect. It isn't often you can do that, that that happens, and really I suppose I've got you to thank. *(He bends forward and pats* STELLA'*s arm)* Thanks.

There is a pause. STELLA *rises and moves behind the sofa.*

He reminds me of a bloke I went to school with. Hawkins. Honestly, he reminded me of Hawkins. Hawkins was an opera fan, too. So's what's-his-name. I'm a bit of an opera fan myself. Always kept it a dead secret. I might go along with your bloke to the opera one night. *(He rises and moves to the radiogram)* He says he can always get free seats. *(He takes the record from the turntable and puts it in its sleeve)* He knows quite a few of that crowd. Maybe I can track old Hawkins down and take him along, too. *(He puts the record in the record cabinet)* He's a very cultivated bloke, your bloke, quite a considerable intelligence at work there, I thought. He's got a collection of Chinese pots stuck on the wall, must have cost at least fifteen hundred a piece. Well, you can't help noticing that sort of thing. I mean, you couldn't say he wasn't a man of taste. He's brimming over with it. Well, I suppose he must have struck you the same way. No, really, I think I should thank you, rather than anything else. After two years of marriage it looks as though, by accident, you've opened up a whole new world to me.

The lights on the room right fade and come up on the room and hall left. It is night. BILL *enters left from the kitchen, carrying a tray with cheese, crisps, snacks, etc., some clean glasses and a transistor radio, which is playing. He puts the tray on the table, transfers the*

*glasses to the sideboard, pours himself a drink, goes to
the table, takes a crisp and eats it.*

JAMES *enters right in the street, crosses to the front door
and rings the bell.* **BILL** *goes into the hall and opens the
door.* **JAMES** *comes into the hall, hangs up his coat, goes
into the living-room and looks at the vases on the wall
up left.* **BILL** *closes the door, goes into the living-room,
moves to the sideboard and pours a drink for* **JAMES**.
The lights come up on the telephone-box.

HARRY *enters left and goes into the box. The lights in
the box come on. The telephone right, rings. The radio
music softens. The lights come up on the room right.*

STELLA *enters right, carrying the cat. She puts the cat
on the sofa, goes to the telephone and lifts the receiver.*

STELLA *(into the telephone)* Hullo?

HARRY's *voice is heard.*

HARRY *(through the telephone)* Is that you, James?

STELLA What? No, it isn't. Who's this?

HARRY Where's James?

STELLA He's out.

HARRY Out? Oh, well, all right. I'll be straight round.

STELLA What are you talking about? Who are you?

HARRY Don't go out.

HARRY *replaces the receiver, leaves the telephone-box
and exits up right. The light in the box goes out.* **STELLA**
*replaces her receiver then sits on the sofa. The lights on
the telephone-box fades. The lights on the room right
fade to half.* **BILL**, *in the room left, hands a drink to*
JAMES. *They clink glasses and drink.*

JAMES You know something? You remind me of a chap I knew once. Hawkins. Yes. He was quite a tall lad.

BILL Tall, was he?

JAMES Yes.

BILL Now why would I remind you of him?

JAMES He was quite a card.

BILL *(after a pause)* Tall, was he?

JAMES That's—what he was.

BILL Well, you're not short.

JAMES I'm not tall.

BILL Quite broad.

JAMES That doesn't make me tall.

BILL I never said it did.

JAMES Well, what are you saying?

BILL Nothing.

JAMES I wouldn't exactly say I was broad, either.

BILL Well, you only see yourself in the mirror, don't you?

JAMES That's good enough for me.

BILL They're deceptive.

JAMES Mirrors?

BILL Very.

JAMES Have you got one?

BILL What?

JAMES A mirror.

BILL There's one right in front of you.

JAMES So there is. *(He moves down centre and looks out front, presumably into a mirror assumed to be over the fireplace)* Come here. You look in it, too.

BILL moves to left of JAMES. They look together and then JAMES goes first to the left of the mirror and then to the right, looking at BILL's reflection.

I don't think mirrors are deceptive. *(He moves to the chair down left and sits)*

BILL offers JAMES a cigarette from the box on the sideboard. JAMES refuses. BILL sits on the chair right of the table. The lights on the room left and the hall fade to half. The lights on the room right come up to full. A doorbell rings off right. The radio music fades out.

STELLA rises and exits right.

STELLA *(offstage)* Yes?

HARRY *(offstage)* I wonder if I might have a word with you? No need to be alarmed. May I come in?

The front door is heard to close.

How do you do? My name's Kane. In here?

STELLA Yes.

HARRY and STELLA enter right.

HARRY *(crossing to left of the sofa)* What a beautiful lamp.

STELLA *(standing right of the sofa)* What can I do for you?

HARRY Do you know Bill Lloyd?

STELLA *(after a pause)* No.

HARRY Oh, you don't?

STELLA No.

HARRY You don't know him personally?

STELLA I don't, no.

HARRY I found him in a slum, you know, by accident. Just happened to be in a slum one day and there he was. I realized he had talent straight away. I gave him a roof, gave him a job and he came up trumps. We've been close friends for years.

There is a pause. STELLA *moves to the radiogram and takes a cigarette from the box on it.*

STELLA Oh, yes?

HARRY You know of him, of course, don't you, by repute? He's a dress designer.

STELLA I know of him.

HARRY You're both dress designers.

STELLA Yes.

HARRY You don't belong to the *Rags and Bags Club*, do you?

STELLA The what?

HARRY The *Rags and Bags Club*. I thought I might have seen you down there.

STELLA No, I don't know it.

HARRY *(moving to* STELLA *and lighting her cigarette)* Shame. You'd like it. *(He pauses)* Yes. *(He pauses and moves above the coffee-table)* I've come about your husband.

STELLA Oh?

HARRY Yes. He's been bothering Bill recently, with some fantastic story.

STELLA I know about it.

HARRY Oh, you know?

STELLA Yes. *(She sits on the sofa)* I'm very sorry.

HARRY *(sitting in the armchair)* Well, it's really been rather disturbing. I mean, the boy has his work to get on with. This sort of thing spoils his concentration.

STELLA I'm sorry. It's—very unfortunate.

HARRY It is.

There is a pause.

STELLA I can't understand it. We've been happily married for two years, you see. I've—been away before, you know—showing dresses, here and there—my husband runs the business. But it's never happened before.

HARRY What hasn't?

STELLA Well, that my husband has suddenly invented such a fantastic story, for no reason at all.

HARRY That's what I said it was. I said it was a fantastic story.

STELLA It is.

HARRY That's what I said and that's what Bill says. We both think it's a fantastic story.

STELLA I mean, Mr Lloyd was in Leeds, but I hardly saw him, even though we were both staying in the same hotel. I never met him or spoke to him—and then my husband suddenly accused me of... It's really been very distressing.

HARRY Yes. What do you think the answer is? Do you think your husband—doesn't trust you, or something?

STELLA Of course he does—he's just not been very well lately, actually—overwork.

HARRY That's bad. Still, you know what it's like in our business. Why don't you take him on a long holiday? South of France.

STELLA Yes. I'm very sorry that Mr Lloyd has had to put up with all this, anyway.

HARRY *(rising)* Oh, what a beautiful kitten, what a really beautiful kitten. Kitty, kitty, kitty—what do you call her?

Come here, kitty—kitty. *(He sits beside* STELLA *on the sofa and pets and nuzzles the cat)*

The lights on the room right fade to half. The lights on the room left and the hall come up to full. BILL *and* JAMES *are still seated with their drinks.*

BILL Hungry?

JAMES No.

BILL Biscuit?

JAMES I'm not hungry.

BILL I've got some olives.

JAMES Really?

BILL Like one?

JAMES No, thanks.

BILL Why not?

JAMES I don't like them.

BILL *(after a pause)* Don't like olives? *(He pauses)* What on earth have you got against olives?

JAMES *(after a pause)* I detest them.

BILL Really?

JAMES It's the smell I hate.

BILL *(after a pause)* Cheese? I've got a splendid cheese knife. *(He picks up a cheese knife from the tray, rises and moves to* JAMES*)* Look. Don't you think it's splendid?

JAMES Is it sharp?

BILL Try it. Hold the blade. It won't cut you. Not if you handle it properly. Not if you grasp it firmly up to the hilt.

JAMES does not touch the knife. BILL *stands holding it.*

The lights on the room right come up to full.

HARRY *(rising)* Well, good-bye. I'm glad we've had our little chat.

STELLA *(rising)* Yes.

HARRY It's all quite clear now.

STELLA I'm glad.

HARRY Oh, Mr Lloyd asked me if I would give you his best wishes—and sympathies.

> **STELLA** *and* **HARRY** *exit right.*

> *(offstage)* Good-bye.

> *The front door is heard to close.*

> **STELLA** *re-enters right, takes a cigarette from the box on the radiogram, lights it, then lies on the sofa, rests her head back and is still. The lights on the room right fade to half.*

BILL What are you frightened of?

JAMES *(rising and crossing to right)* What's that?

BILL What?

JAMES I thought it was thunder.

BILL *(moving to left of* **JAMES***)* Why are you frightened of holding this blade?

JAMES I'm not frightened. I was just thinking of the thunder last week, when you and my wife were in Leeds.

BILL Oh, not again, surely? I thought we'd left all that behind. Surely we have? You're not still worried about that, are you?

JAMES Oh, no. Just nostalgia, that's all.

BILL Surely the wound heals when you know the truth, doesn't it? I mean, when the truth is verified. I would have thought it did.

JAMES *(moving to the table)* Of course.

BILL *(following* JAMES*)* What's there left to think about? It's a thing regretted, never to be repeated. No past, no future. Do you see what I mean? *(He moves down centre)* You're a chap who's been married for two years, aren't you, happily?

HARRY *enters up right in the street and crosses to the front door.*

There's a bond of iron between you and your wife. It can't be corroded by a trivial thing like this. I've apologized, she's apologized. Honestly, what more can you want?

There is a pause. JAMES *looks at* BILL, *who smiles.* HARRY *comes quietly into the hall, and remains there unnoticed by the others.*

JAMES Nothing.

BILL Every woman is bound to have an outburst of—wild sensuality at one time or another. That's the way I look at it, anyway. It's part of their nature. Even though it may be the kind of sensuality of which you yourself have never been the fortunate recipient. What? *(He laughs)* That is a husband's fate, I suppose. Mind you, I think it's the system that's at fault, not you. Perhaps she'll never need to do it again, who knows?

JAMES *picks up a fruit knife from the table and runs his finger along the blade.*

JAMES This is fairly sharp.

BILL What do you mean?

JAMES Come on.

BILL I beg your pardon?

JAMES Come on. You've got that one. I've got this one.

BILL What about it?

JAMES I get a bit tired of words sometimes, don't you? Let's have a game. For fun.

BILL What sort of game?

JAMES Let's have a mock duel.

BILL I don't want a mock duel, thank you.

JAMES Of course you do. Come on. First one who's touched is a sissy.

BILL This is all rather unsubtle, don't you think?

JAMES Not in the least. Come on, into first position.

BILL I thought we were friends.

JAMES Of course we're friends. What on earth's the matter with you? I'm not going to kill you. It's just a game, that's all. We're playing a game. You're not windy, are you?

BILL I think it's silly,

JAMES I say, you're a bit of a spoilsport, aren't you?

BILL I'm putting my knife down, anyway. *(He puts his knife on the table and moves down left)*

JAMES Well, I'll pick it up. *(He picks up the cheese knife, moves down left centre and faces* **BILL***)*

BILL Now you've got two.

JAMES I've got another one in my hip pocket.

BILL *(after a pause)* What do you do, swallow them?

JAMES Do you?

There is a pause. They stare at each other.

(suddenly) Go on! Swallow it! *(He throws the cheese knife at* **BILL**'*s face)*

BILL *throws up his hand to protect his face and catches the knife by the blade. It cuts his hand.*

BILL Ow!

JAMES Well caught! What's the matter? *(He moves to* BILL *and examines his hand)* Let's have a look. Ah, yes. Now you've got a scar on your hand. You didn't have one before, did you?

HARRY *comes into the room.*

HARRY *(moving between* JAMES *and* BILL*)* What have you done, nipped your hand? Let's have a look. *(To* JAMES*)* Only a little nip, isn't it? It's his own fault for not ducking. I must have told him dozens of times, you know, that if someone throws a knife at you the silliest thing you can do is to catch it. You're bound to hurt yourself, unless it's made of rubber. The safest thing to do is duck. You're Mr Horne?

JAMES That's right.

HARRY I'm so glad to meet you. *(He shakes hands with* JAMES*)* My name's Harry Kane. Bill been looking after you all right? I asked him to see that you stayed until I got back, so glad you could spare the time. What are we drinking? Whisky? Let's fill you up. *(He collects* JAMES' *glass, goes to the sideboard and pours two drinks)*

BILL *sits on the chair down left.*

You and your wife run that little boutique down the road, don't you? *(He crosses to* JAMES*)* Funny we've never met, living so close, all in the same trade, eh? *(He hands* JAMES *his glass)* Here you are. Got one, Bill? Where's your glass? This one? *(He collects* BILL*'s glass, refills it and hands it to him)* Here—you are. Oh, stop rubbing your hand, for goodness' sake. It's only a cheese knife. *(He collects his own drink and turns to* JAMES*)* Well, Mr Horne, all the very best. Here's wishing us all health, happiness and prosperity in the time to come, not forgetting your wife, of course. Healthy minds in healthy bodies. Cheers. *(He drinks then sits left of the table)*

JAMES *drinks.*

By the way, I've just seen your wife, what a beautiful kitten she has, you should see it, Bill, it's all white. We had a very pleasant chat, your wife and I. Listen—old chap—can I be quite blunt with you?

JAMES Of course.

HARRY Your wife—you see—made a little tiny confession to me. I think I can use that word. *(He pauses)*

BILL *is sucking his hand.*

What she confessed was—that she'd made the whole thing up. She'd made the whole damn thing up. For some odd reason of her own. They never met, you know, Bill and your wife, they never even spoke. This is what Bill says, and this is now what your wife admits. They had nothing whatever to do with each other, they don't know each other. Women are very strange. But I suppose you know more about them than I do, she's your wife. If I were you I'd go home and knock her over the head with a saucepan and tell her not to make up such stories again.

There is a long pause.

JAMES She made the whole thing up, eh?

HARRY I'm afraid she did.

JAMES I see. Well, thanks very much for telling me.

HARRY I thought it would be clearer for you, coming from someone completely outside the whole matter.

JAMES Yes. Thank you.

HARRY Isn't that so, Bill?

BILL Oh, quite so. I don't even know the woman. Wouldn't know her if I saw her. Pure fantasy.

JAMES How's your hand?

BILL Not bad.

JAMES Isn't it strange that you confirmed the whole of her story?

BILL It amused me to do so.

JAMES Oh?

BILL Yes. You amused me. You wanted me to confirm it. It amused me to do so.

There is a pause.

HARRY Bill's a slum boy, you see, he's got a slum sense of humour. That's why I never take him along with me to parties. Because he's got a slum mind. I have nothing against slum minds *per se,* you understand, nothing at all. There's a certain kind of slum mind which is perfectly all right in a slum, but when this kind of slum mind gets out of the slum it sometimes persists, you see, it rots everything. That's what Bill is. There's something faintly putrid about him, don't you find? Like a slug. There's nothing wrong with slugs, in their place, but he's a slum slug, there's nothing wrong with slum slugs in their place, but this one won't keep his place, he crawls all over the walls of nice houses, leaving slime, don't you, boy? He confirms stupid, sordid little stories just to amuse himself, while everyone else has to run round in circles to get to the root of the matter and smooth the whole thing out. All he can do is sit and suck his bloody hand and decompose like the filthy putrid slum slug he is. *(He rises and moves to* **JAMES***)* What about another whisky, Horne?

JAMES *(moving up centre)* No, I think I must be off, now.

HARRY Oh?

JAMES Well, I'm glad to hear that nothing did happen. Great relief to me.

HARRY It must be.

JAMES My wife's not been very well lately, actually. Overwork.

HARRY That's bad. Still, you know what it's like in our business.

JAMES Best thing to do is take her on a long holiday, I think.

HARRY South of France.

JAMES The Greek islands.

HARRY Sun's essential, of course.

JAMES I know. Bermuda.

HARRY Perfect.

JAMES Well, thanks very much, Mr Kane, for clearing my mind. I don't think I'll mention it when I get home. Take her out for a drink or something. Forget all about it.

HARRY Better hurry up. It's nearly closing time.

JAMES moves and stands over BILL.

JAMES I'm very sorry I cut your hand. You're lucky you caught it, of course. Otherwise it might have cut your mouth. Still, it's not too bad, is it? *(He pauses)* Look—I really think I ought to apologize for this silly story my wife made up. The fault is really all hers, and mine, for believing her. You're not to blame for taking it as you did. The whole thing must have been an impossible burden for you. What do you say we shake hands, as a testimony of my good will? *(He extends his hand)*

BILL rubs his hand and does not extend it.

HARRY Come on, Billy, I think we've had enough of this stupidity, don't you?

JAMES looks sharply at BILL.

BILL I never touched her—we sat—in the lounge, on a sofa—for two hours—talked—we talked about it—we didn't—move from the lounge—never went to her room—just talked— about what we would do—if we did go to her room—two hours—we never touched—we just talked about it...

There is a long silence.

JAMES goes out by the front door and exits up right. BILL, still sitting down left, sucks his hand. HARRY sits right of the table. The lights on the room left and the hall fade to half. The lights on the room right come up to full. STELLA, with the cat, is lying on the sofa. The front door off right is heard to slam.

JAMES enters right, stands behind the sofa and looks at STELLA. There is a silence. STELLA strokes the cat.

JAMES You didn't do anything, did you? *(He pauses)* He wasn't in your room. You just talked about it, in the lounge. *(He pauses)* That's the truth, isn't it? *(He pauses)* You just sat and talked about what you would do, if you went to your room. That's what you did. *(He pauses)* Didn't you? *(He pauses and sits in the armchair)* That's the truth—isn't it?

STELLA looks at JAMES, neither confirming nor denying. Her face is friendly, sympathetic. The lights on the room right fade to half. There is a long pause. The four figures are still, in the half light, then the lights dim to blackout as—

The curtain falls.

FURNITURE AND PROPERTY LIST

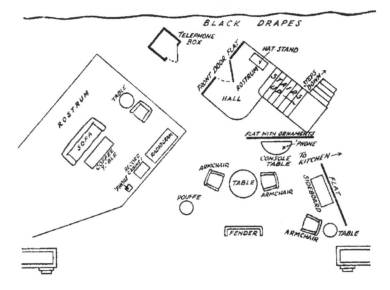

On stage: Harry's house left:

    Round table. *On it:* white cloth, bowl of fruit with grapes and fruit knife

    2 carver chairs

    Sideboard. *On it:* tray, 4 glasses, various bottles, ashtray, silver candlesticks, box with cigarettes, matches

    Low-backed fireside chair

    Occasional table (down left) *On it:* magazines

    Console table (up centre) *On it:* telephone

    On wall behind console table: brackets with figurines

    Pouffe (right)

    Carpet on floor

    Fender and fire-irons (down centre)

    In hall: hatstand. *In it:* umbrella, cane, Bill's coat

    On front door: practical doorbell

James' flat right:

    Sofa. *On it:* cushions

    Low coffee-table. *On it:* ashtray, cup of coffee

    Armchair

    Occasional-table. *On it:* table-lamp

Radiogram. *On it:* ashtray, box with cigarettes,
matches, Stella's gloves, purse, and handbag.
In handbag: bracelet, purfume atomizer
Record cabinet. *In it:* records
Telephone (down centre)
Telephone-box: *In it:* telephone and coin box

Off stage: Coat (**Stella**)
Cigarette (**James**)
Tray. *On it:* 2 glasses fruit juice, toast rack, 2 cups,
2 saucers, 2 teaspoons, pot of tea, jug of milk,
sugar basin (**Bill**)
Magazines (**Bill**)
White Persian kitten (**Stella**)
Tray. *On it:* breakfast for two, newspaper (**Harry**)
Tray. *On it:* pot of coffee, milk, sugar, 2 cups, 2
saucers, 2 spoons, plate of biscuits (**Stella**)
Tray. *On it:* cheese board with cheese and knife,
cheese biscuits, plate of celery, carrot and olives,
clean glasses, dish of crisps (**Bill**)
Transistor radio (**Bill**)

Personal: **Stella**: handbag
James: wallet

LIGHTING PLOT

Property fittings required: table-lamp

The Main Acting Areas are a room right, a room left, an entrance hall up left centre and a telephone-box up left centre

To open: The rooms in darkness. Moonlight effect in street up left centre. Telephone-box interior light on. Hall area lit

Cue 1	**Harry** switches on lights	(Page 2)
	Bring up lights on room left	
Cue 2	**James** leaves telephone-box	(Page 3)
	Snap out telephone-box light	
	Fade out street moonlight	
Cue 3	**Harry** switches off lights	(Page 3)
	Fade out lights on room left and hall	
	Bring in lights on room right for	
	daylight effect	
Cue 4	**Stella** exits and **James** cont. regarding...	(Page 4)
	Fade lights on room right to half	
	Bring up lights on room left and hall	
	for daylight effect	
Cue 5	**James** exits right	(Page 4)
	Fade lights on room right	
Cue 6	**Harry**: "No, thank you."	(Page 6)
	Bring up lights on telephone-box to half	
Cue 7	**James** enters telephone-box	(Page 6)
	Snap in box light	
Cue 8	**James** leaves telephone-box	(Page 7)
	Snap out telephone-box light	
Cue 9	**James** and **Harry** exit	(Page 9)
	Fade lights on room left	
	Fade lights on telephone-box	

*Bring up lights on room right for
   moonlight effect*

Cue 10 Front door right slams   (Page 9)
        Snap on hall light off right

Cue 11 **Stella** switches on table-lamp   (Page 9)
        Snap in lights on room right to half

Cue 12 **Stella** exits right   (Page 9)
        Bring up lights on room and hall left

Cue 13 **Stella** lies on sofa   (Page 10)
        Fade hall light right

Cue 14 **James** rings doorbell   (Page 10)
        Dim lights on room right a little

Cue 15 **Stella** exits right   (Page 12)
        *Fade lights and table-lamp in room
          right*

Cue 16 **Bill**: "Lying."   (Page 20)
        Blackout

Cue 17 Follows above cue   (Page 20)
        *Bring up lights on room right, room
          left and hall*

Cue 18 **Bill** and **Harry** exit up the stairs   (Page 24)
        Fade lights on room left and hall

Cue 19 **James**: "...world to me."   (Page 27)
        *Fade lights on room right and bring up
          lights on room and hall left*

Cue 20 **James** enters by front door   (Page 28)
        Bring up lights on telephone-box

Cue 21 **Harry** enters telephone-box   (Page 28)
        Snap in light in telephone-box

Cue 22 Telephone right rings   (Page 28)
        Bring up lights on room right

Cue 23	**Harry** leaves telephone-box	(Page 28)
	Snap out light in telephone-box	
	Fade lights on telephone-box	
	Fade lights on room right to half	

Cue 24   **Bill** sits   (Page 30)
Fade lights on room left and hall to
   half
Bring up lights on room right to full

Cue 25   **Harry** sits on the sofa   (Page 33)
Fade lights on room right to half
Bring up lights on room left and hall to
   full

Cue 26   **Bill**: "...to the hilt."   (Page 33)
Bring up lights on room right to full

Cue 27   **Stella** lies on sofa   (Page 34)
Fade lights on room right to half

Cue 28   **James** exits   (Page 41)
Fade lights on room left to half
Bring up lights on room right to full

Cue 29   **James**: "That's the truth—isn't it?"   (Page 41)
Fade lights on room right to half

Cue 30   Follows above cue after a long pause   (Page 41)
Dim all lights to blackout

EFFECTS PLOT

Cue 1	At rise of curtain *Telephone left rings*	(Page 1)
Cue 2	**Stella** exits *Front door right slams*	(Page 4)
Cue 3	**Harry** exits *Telephone left rings*	(Page 7)
Cue 4	**James** and **Harry** exit *Front door right slams*	(Page 9)
Cue 5	**Stella** switches on radiogram *Cool jazz music*	(Page 9)
Cue 6	**James** rings doorbell *Fade music to out*	(Page 10)
Cue 7	**Bill**: "Lying." *Sound of church bells*	(Page 20)
Cue 8	After lights come up *Fade bells*	(Page 20)
Cue 9	**James**: "...them or not." *Telephone left rings*	(Page 22)
Cue 10	**Bill** enters with transistor radio *Radio music*	(Page 27)
Cue 11	**Harry** enters telephone-box *Telephone right rings* *Reduce volume of radio music to half*	(Page 28)
Cue 12	The lights come up on room right *Doorbell rings off right* *Radio music fades out*	(Page 30)
Cue 13	**Harry**: "May I come in?" *Door closes off right*	(Page 30)

CPSIA information can be obtained
at www.ICGtesting.com
Printed in the USA
BVHW01s2231041217
501906BV00019B/1262/P

9 780573 020360